TUPPENNY

The arrival of cinemas and film-making
in Swadlincote

Graham Nutt

An illustration from an advertising card for the 'Empire Picture Palace', West Street, Swadlincote. Circa 1913. (M. McCann).

Front cover:
The 'Empire Theatre', West Street, Swadlincote. (M. McCann).

Rear cover:
Empire advertisment (G. Nutt).

© Graham Nutt, Trent Valley Publications, 1992.
All rights reserved. No part of this book may be reproduced or transmitted in any form or by any means, electronic or mechanical, including photocopying, recording by any information storage or retrieval system, without the permission of the publisher and author in writing.

ISBN 0-948131-33-0

Trent Valley Publications

P.O. Box 9
Burton-on-Trent
Staffs
DE15 9QU

Acknowledgements

I wish to place on record my gratitude to the following people for the help and encouragement they have given me in preparing this book. Dorothy Jamieson, Bert Holland, Sam Jones, Minnie Nutt, Fred Illsley, Edith Nicholson, Sally Mewis, Morris McCann, Peter White, Andy Parker, Jaqueline Shorthouse, Joe Storer, Brian Robinson, Alan Freeman, Len Jones, Harry Robinson, Roy Taylor, Jim Smith, Tony Gardner (Richardsons Chemists), Burton Mail Ltd., The Staff of Swadlincote Library.

Other sources of information...
Seventy Years a Showman by 'Lord' George Sanger
Published by MacGibbon and Kee.
The Aberdeen Journal
Burton Evening Gazette
Burton Chronicle
Burton Observer
Burton Daily Mail

Introduction

"They made a film in Swad you know. About a poacher. Charlie Hextall was in it." I had heard the story several times from different sources. Once again the tale had cropped up in conversation as I enjoyed a drink in the 'Barley Mow', next to Gresley Common. "If the film still exists, imagine the local scenes and characters from the past that must be on it," remarked one of my drinking companions.

The subject would have drifted away as quickly as it came, but for a remark from an elderly gentleman sitting nearby. "Arl tell yu who made that film. It were master Lawrence outa Weston Strate".

Curiosity took over and I went in search of this celluloid antiquity, but to no avail. What did emerge were photographs and stories from the descendants of those who had been the pioneers of the cinema in Swadlincote.

It also transpired that more than one film was made in and around the town!

SWADLINCOTE Circa 1905
(Not to scale)

Labels on map:
- James Woodwards Works (Wraggs)
- Wilsons Ground
- 2nd proposed site for Empire Theatre
- 1st proposed site for Empire Theatre
- Stanhope Arms
- Market Inn
- Hunters Stores
- Site of Alexandra Rink
- Nags Head Hotel
- Bank Passage
- Final Site for Empire Theatre
- Sharpes Reservoir
- Tills Printing Works
- Sharpes Works
- Sabines Ground
- Market Hall
- Granville Hotel
- Wesleyan Chapel

A Gathering of Travellers

It was the late 1700's. The young man had spent several years helping on his father's large Wiltshire farm, and was apprenticed to a local toolmaker. He had been thrifty, saving enough money to visit friends in London. On his 18th birthday he was granted leave to make his journey and stay in the capital.

In his best clothes, he boarded a wagon at the village of Tisbury near the edge of Salisbury Plain, waved goodbye to family and friends, and headed for the Metropolis.

After arriving in London, he set out on foot towards his destination, which lay over the other side of London Bridge. As he reached the far side of the bridge there was a commotion, accompanied by shouts of 'Press! Press!'

He tried to avoid the uproar, but within half an hour the 'Press Gang' took him aboard a government tender on the Thames, along with over 100 other groaning, sore-headed individuals.

Ten long years in the British Navy found him at Trafalgar aboard Admiral Lord Nelson's flagship, H.M.S. Victory. During the battle he received a severe scalp wound and several broken ribs and lost three fingers. Since the Service then regarded him as an invalid, they released the reluctant sailor, granting him an annual pension of £10.

On his return to his Wiltshire home the welcome was anything but warm. His mother and father had passed away, and his four brothers, who had occupations which allowed them to mix with the upper echelons of society, gave him the cold shoulder. They made it clear that the last person they wished to be troubled with was a maimed ex-sailor, brother or no brother.

The outcast made his way to Bristol where a fair was being held. Perhaps he was hoping to be hired, but this did not happen.

While serving King and Country he had befriended two Jewish brothers by the name of Hart who had been 'press ganged' at the same time. They taught him several juggling and conjuring tricks.

During his visit to the fair he invested cash in various 'props' of the magical trade and also a 'peep show'. With this newly acquired equipment he set out on the road as a travelling showman.

Hard work brought prosperity. He married, and, in addition to his travelling home, bought a house near the market place in Newbury, Berkshire. It was here, on December 23rd, 1827, their sixth child was born. It was a son, christened George.

Of all James Sanger's children, George was the one who took the family trade beyond his parents' wildest dreams.

The circus of 'Lord' George Sanger was to become renowned

throughout the world and was patronised by the Royal Families of many countries, including our own.

The paths of this guru of the travelling show were to intertwine with many others of nomadic occupations...

In 1860 George Sanger's Circus visited Plymouth but not in the usual format. Plymouth Hoe was the venue for the spectacular, which boasted three circus rings, and two platforms, with simultaneous performances.

Around the perimeter was a fair made up of over 100 travelling showmen and their families. Sanger allowed them all free-standing, but the public paid admission to the showground! It was a huge success.

Among the encircling travellers was the Lawrence family, who rambled annually from coast to coast across southern England. Like many others they had found Sanger's offer of a free pitch one they could not refuse.

Among their entertainments was a 'Lantern Show', the predecessor of the slide and movie Projector.

On the afternoon of the last day of the circus's stay at Plymouth, nine-year old Edwin Lawrence slipped away to watch the impressive Sanger presentation. He was a good looking child, with lightbrown curly hair, strong and his skin coloured by the seasons. Behind his bright eyes lay a shrewd, alert mind.

He watched for as long as he dare. If father found him missing, on his return he would be told to read the plaque in their caravan home: 'THEM THAT WORK, EAT'.

★ ★ ★

By sunrise the multitude of amusement-makers had left. The expertise of dismantling and loading, along with hard work and sweat in the early hours of morning, was a sight few static mortals seldom witnessed or appreciated. The overnight disappearing act of the travelling show and fairground had been performed.

Sanger and entourage moved to their next venue. While the Lawrence family, along with a small group of other travellers made tracks across the Devonshire countryside.

It was a hard but enjoyable existence. Young Edwin experienced the flavours of life in large cities, country towns, villages and fishing ports scattered along the south coast. But his early years were also spiced with death.

A small band of travellers was encamped in the countryside north of Plymouth. Edwin, along with other children, was playing on the outskirts of the settlement. The horses were pegged out and grazing on suitable pasture nearby, women were preparing food over open campfires.

Suddenly there was a tremendous explosion, followed by silence punctuated only by the crackle of burning timber. The home of the Lawrence family had been destroyed. Their dazed associates did all they could to save the caravan and those inside it, but to no avail.

Edwin's father and eldest brother had been making fireworks. A mistake, by one or both of them, had taken their lives and destroyed their home. The survivors of the family were taken in and cared for by their travelling companions.

Edwin was a studious child. Quick to learn to read and write, he also showed a talent for sketching and painting. He was fascinated by the photography booths which were appearing on the fairgrounds.

By the 1880's he was married and based at Forest Gate in north-east London. He was now travelling further north and across the Midlands. His academic and technical ability was admired by many other travelling showmen.

Edwin became a first rate photographer. He created his own scenes and backdrops, and produced glass slides, which he colour tinted, presenting them on his 'Magic Lantern Show'. Marionettes were also a favourite, and Lawrence's Marionettes were a regular attraction at Nottingham Goose Fair.

On the left of this photograph is the marionette show of Edwin Lawrence. The location is thought to be Oxford St. Giles Fair, circa 1880. (D. Jamieson).

Edwin Lawrence's Bioscope Show, awaits the finishing touches in preparation for the 1906 Nottingham Goose Fair. (D. Jamieson).

While Edwin was covering many of the larger fairs and touring into the Midlands, Sanger's Circus was travelling everywhere. On one of Sanger's many visits to north-east England in the 1890's, The Raynor Troupé of Marvellous Grotesques were part of his presentation. After the show had finished, Raynor and his men made their way back to their quarters to find a young boy sitting on the steps to the caravan.

A smile spread across Jack Raynor's face. He had lost count of how many times Tommy Oliphant had run away from home to try to join them. The youngster's elder brother, who was part of the Raynor act, threw up his arms in despair.

Nine-year-old Tommy made his usual fervent plea to be allowed to travel with the Raynors, and Jack Raynor put forward his usual proposal.

If the youngster was able to leap off the bottom tread of the caravan steps, perform a mid-air somersault, then land on his feet, he would receive a half crown piece. Also, providing the others in the troupe approved, he would be allowed to join them, and eventually appear in the act.

Tommy was ready. He had been practising since his last confrontation with Raynor. The boy launched himself into the air, carried out the ariel manouvre and followed it with a perfect touchdown. The onlookers applauded!

Jack Raynor honoured the bargain.

Running away to join the circus was a dream to many young people. For Tommy it had come true. It had released him from his back street home in Tyneside and a future working in the shipyards with his father.

After joining the Raynors he was educated in the art of make-up, far beyond the borders of being ridiculous, and taught the twists and turns of becoming a contortionist and acrobat.

By the latter half of the 1890's Tommy was an accomplished member of the act. In 1898 Sanger had been sent a Royal Command for his circus to appear on the 17th June, at Balmoral Castle, in the presence of Queen Victoria.

The Aberdeen Journal of the 18th June carried a report of the spectacle and stated: "The Queen expressed her great delight with the entertainment, especially mentioning the wire performers, and 'The Raynor Troupe'".

Thereafter the troupe's name appeared in programmes as: 'The Royal Raynor's'.

Three of the Raynor Troupe, Jack Raynor centre, Tommy Oliphant (alias Raynor) on the right. The gentleman on the left is believed to be Tommy's elder brother. This photograph is from a set of three, showing the troupe in various action shots and ridiculous forms of make-up. These photographs were eventually mounted in a large frame, and were displayed in the entrance area of the 'Alexandra Palace of Varieties' during its early years. (D. Jamieson).

𝒱.   𝑅.

Balmoral Castle, 17th June, 1898.

Lord George Sanger's Circus Company

BY SPECIAL COMMAND
OF
Her Most Gracious Majesty Queen Victoria.

PERFORMANCE COMMENCING AT 3.30.

...PROGRAMME...

1. Overture by the Magnificent Band, conductor, E. Scholz.
2. Harry Austin will Ride, Drive, and Manage Four Beautiful Coloured Horses.
3. Acrobatic Violinists, by the Bros. Crippi.
4. The Wonderful Clairvoyant and Talking Horse. Introduced by Herr Lancelot. Trained by Lord George Sanger.
5. Mdlle. Ida Evilo in her Daring Trapeze Performance.
6. Performing Horse and Pony, trained and introduced by Herr Nimsi.
7. The Toledas in their Extraordinary Wire Show, and Mdlle. Yetta.
8. Beautiful Menage Horse, "Lord Chieftain," introduced by Mons. Arnold.
9. Mdlle. Lilian, the Charming Equestrienne. (Clown, the Great James Holloway).
10. The Eccentric Mule.
11. The Bros. Holloway. Extraordinary Performance on the Double Ladders.
12. Mdlle. Violetta in her Graceful Trotting Act. (Clown the Original Little Sandy).
13. Six Spotted Horses, introduced by Herr Nimsi.
14. The World-Famed Raynor Troupe.
15. Carlo Bianchi, the Barrel King.
16. Harry Austin, as the Newmarket Jockey.
17. The Flying Stellios.
18. The Wonderful Fire-Horse, "Kohinoor."

"GOD SAVE THE QUEEN."

The programme for 'Lord' George Sangers Royal Command Show at Balmoral Castle on 17th June, 1898. The world Famed Raynor Troupé are item 14 in the proceedings. (D. Jamieson).

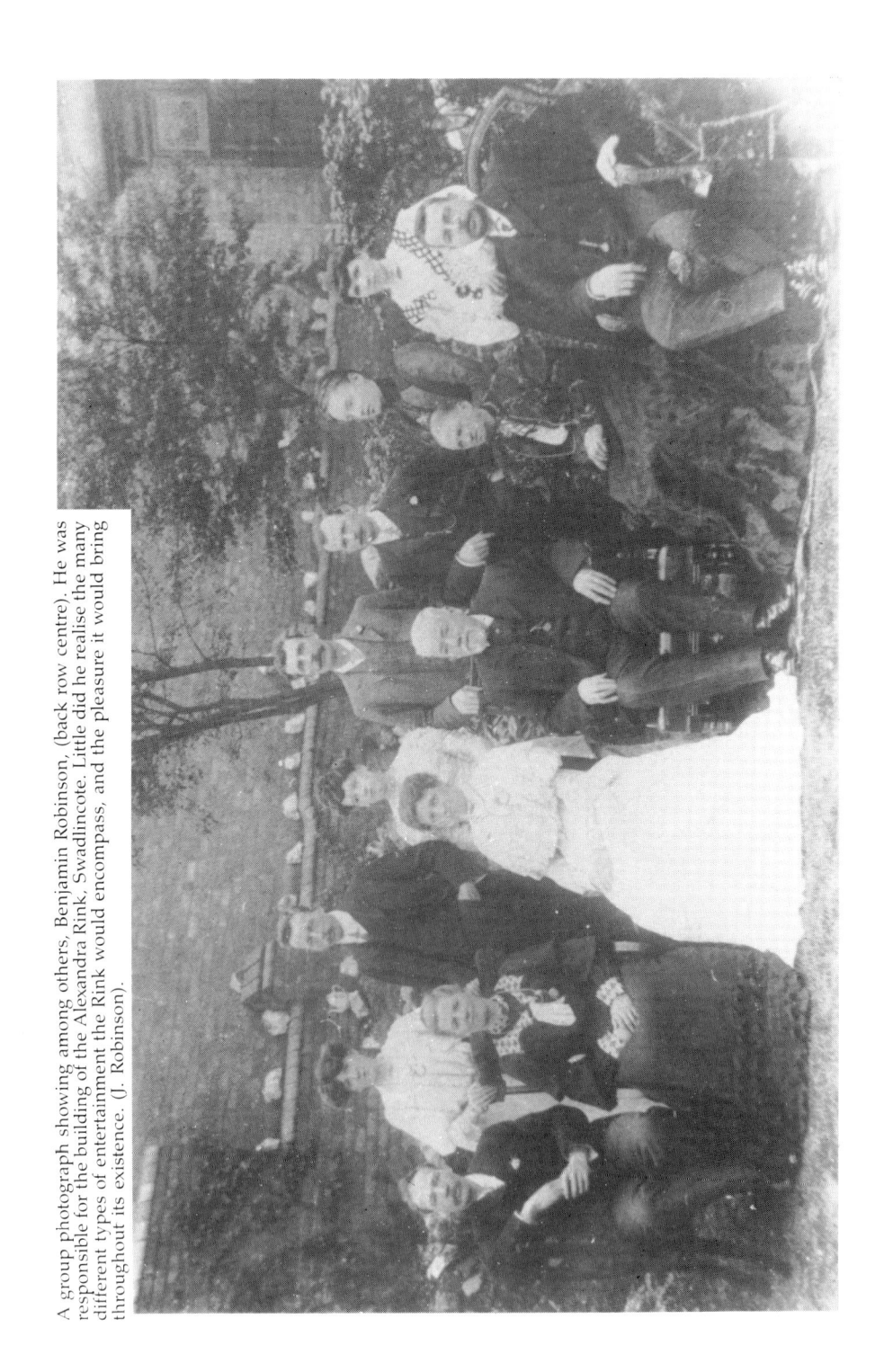

A group photograph showing among others, Benjamin Robinson, (back row centre). He was responsible for the building of the Alexandra Rink, Swadlincote. Little did he realise the many different types of entertainment the Rink would encompass, and the pleasure it would bring throughout its existence. (J. Robinson).

Alexandra Rink, Swadlincote.

(One Minute from Burton & Ashby Light Railway).

The Largest and Best Floor within a radius of Twenty Miles.

Skating Gymkhana.

Thursday, April 21, 1910.

SKATING FROM 7.0 TO 10.30.

Programme.

Usual Skating, etc. until **7.30**, when Races etc. commence.

Two Steps	- -	Partners.
	ALL SKATE.	
Backward Race	- -	Gents.
	ALL SKATE.	
Musical Chairs	- -	Ladies.
	ALL SKATE.	
Musical Chairs	- -	Gents.
	ALL SKATE, with	
Grand Finale		Battle of Confetti.

Ladies' and Gent's Partners, etc. will be introduced into above Programme as time permits.

PRIZES WILL BE AWARDED FOR EACH EVENT

For Fun and Jollity the above Entertainment has not been equalled in the District.

All Skaters are eligible for the various Competitions. No restrictions as to Evening or Fancy Dress.

SEATS PROVIDED FOR THE SPECTATORS.

ADMISSION 6d.   **SKATES, 6d.**

Ward & Till, Printers, Swadlincote.

An early programme for the 'Alexandra Skating Rink'. Even in those days the fine maple floor was gaining a reputation as being one of the best. The proprietors were also quick to point out the close proximity of an up-to date, efficient, public transport system, The Burton and Ashby Light Railway. (P. M. White).

Coal, Clay and Silver Screens

The two little ladies, smartly turned out in elegant white pinafore dresses, white socks and black shoes, were a credit to those who cared for them. Their crisp, bright attire contrasted sharply to the area in which they lived. The lively duo skipped, walked and ran from their home at the top of Wilmot Road, towards Swadlincote High Street.

They paused to look at a new building which was almost finished. It was a huge structure, longer than the Market Hall. Most folk must have felt a tingle of excitement or even pride, that they were to have a roller-skating rink like larger cities and towns. The instigator of the enterprise was Benjamin Robinson, a local sanitary pipe-ware manufacturer.

Minnie and her younger sister Nellie moved on and arrived in 'Swad' at the lower end of Bank Passage. Here they paused, surveying the scene. To the right was Hunter's Stores, with an array of meat hanging around the outside of the window. To the left was the Burton Union Bank Ltd, which gave the name to the pathway they had just travelled. Locals would soon be calling it Rink Passage.

It was Saturday afternoon and the area known as 'The Delph' at the front of the Market Hall was being prepared for the evening market. It

Swadlincote Saturday night market, the many potential customers are spilling over into the road. Many others no doubt, found their way through the doors of The Granville Hotel (left), or The Market Inn (right). There would also be those who would have trouble finding their way out again! (E. Whitehall postcard, G. Nutt).

would be in full swing between the hours of 7pm to 10.30pm, and was something of a spectacle.

Many local shopkeepers and traders would take a pitch, while others from further afield would arrive by train, bringing with them trolleys and hand-carts full of their wares.

There were boiled sweets made while you waited, cries of "Oranges grown in the sunshine, especially for Swadlincote". A medicine man graced the proceedings, sporting a black suit, stetson and western style boots, cracking a huge whip to attract the attention of the crowd. He would then proceed to offer them bottles of elixir which would cure most afflictions from chilblains to the 'Black Death'.

For a short time the youngsters swung around the gas lamp at the bottom of Bank Passage then crossed the road, making their way along High Street, past Goodhead's cake shop and the Stanhope Arms.

Further along they scrutinised the confectionery on James's sweet stall, and savoured the aroma of Mrs. Grice's chips on the pitch next door. They resisted both, and went a few steps further, to the open land on High Street known locally as Wilson's Ground.

Here, in all its glory, stood Swadlincote Hippodrome, better known as Charlie Williams's 'Gaff'.

A combination of wood and canvas, it formed a venue for variety and cinematograph shows. Monetary negotiations between the locals and

An early photograph showing the interior of the 'Alexandra Skating Rink'. The far end was soon to be partitioned off to form the premises of the 'Alexandra Palace of Varieties'. (P. M. White).

travelling showmen had brought an end to the theatre's roaming, and the huge tent had become a more permanent fixture in Swadlincote.

Outside, brightly coloured advertisements informed the public of entertainment for the following week: Alec Godfrey (Comedian), Lydia Raie (Banjo Queen), Ambrose (Comedy Juggler), Horace Sade (Dancer), plus a selection of movie films.

The shows were twice nightly, and there was a weekly change of programme. Prices varied (2d, 4d and 6d), depending on if the customer sat on a wooden bench, a wooden bench with a cushion, or a single upholstered seat.

The power for the lighting was provided by a generator driven by a steam traction engine, which thumped away in the background like the heartbeat of a snoozing giant.

The two girls gazed at the gaudy advertisements on the front of the show, and conversed in excited whispers. Was this where they had planned to go? If so their parents, Sarah and Samuel, would not have allowed them out, as they looked upon the place as a den of iniquity.

Three-o-clock Saturday afternoon at 'The Hippodrome' was matinee time. The twosome each paid their tuppence and filed in with the other patrons.

The smell inside was a mixture of damp canvas, tobacco smoke and sawdust, and the interior was dimly lit by electric lamps. The girls settled themselves at the front on the centre bench, shuffling about in nervous anticipation.

After what seemed like an age, the lady pianist, seated on the right of the screen, launched herself into musical dramatics on the ivories. The gathering looked towards the seemingly gigantic screen.

The projector, in a wooden compartment near the rear of the tent, clattered and flickered into life. Within seconds 'The Hippodrome' clientele were silenced, enthralled by the moving pictures.

Those unable to read the captions on the screen nudged those next to them and whispered: "Wotsitsee, Wotsitsee". (What does it say?) The white haired pianist excelled herself, her accompaniment blending like magic with each scene.

After five or six minutes into the show, the two youngsters were brimming with confidence over their adventure, feeling more like adults than adults.

In the story unfolding on the screen there were the beginnings of a fire. It was obvious the girls and others in the audience were disturbed by this. When a full blown inferno was shown on the screen, fiction and reality were in a blur of utter confusion in the youngster's minds.

They fled from the premises in a state of sheer panic, almost taking the heavy curtains which hung over the cinema entrance with them. The effect of coming from almost total darkness into daylight did nothing to hinder their escape.

There was screeching of steel on steel as they ran across the path of a tram, followed by shouting and cursing from Freddie Fox the driver. The blind, brown pony which pulled the cart of Billy Green, the fishmonger, bolted because of the commotion. A member of the Blankley family, who were competitors of Green's, was quick to react to the situation and swiftly brought the pony and cart to a halt.

Nothing deterred the two girls, who were still in full flight, firmly believing the cinema and Swadlincote were about to be engulfed in flames. But it was not fire that would close Swadlincote Hippodrome.

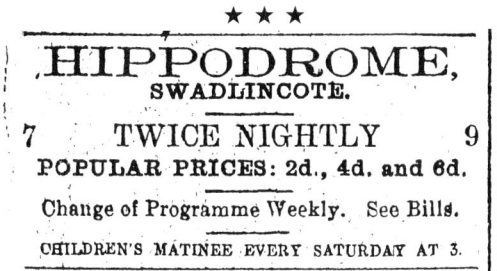

★ ★ ★

HIPPODROME,
SWADLINCOTE.

7   TWICE NIGHTLY   9
POPULAR PRICES: 2d., 4d. and 6d.

Change of Programme Weekly. See Bills.

CHILDREN'S MATINEE EVERY SATURDAY AT 3.

A very basic local newspaper advertisement (November 1910), for 'Swadlincote Hippodrome', better known as 'Charlie Williams Gaff'. Although it was only a canvas and wood structure, it was probably the first permanent cinema in Swadlincote. (Burton Mail Archive).

The cinematograph act of 1910 was the beginning of the end for places such as Charlie Williams's 'Gaff', and the travelling cinemas.

Specially built halls or existing buildings which adhered to the strict fire precautions laid down in the act were the only venues where cinematograph shows could be held. They had to be licensed by the local Councils, and were open to inspection by the police.

As the Swadlincote Hippodrome drifted into extinction, the town witnessed new seeds being sown in the field of entertainment.

According to reports published in Mid-1910, a theatre, which would include facilities for showing movie films, was to be built on land in the vicinity of the gasworks. (The land was owned by Miss Hall of Linden House, Church Street, Swadlincote).

A few weeks later a newspaper report said the site had been changed. It stated that ground opposite the 'Bulls Head' in Swadlincote High Street had been purchased from Walter Jones by The Empire Theatre Company Ltd. of Fleetwood. The company believed this was a better location than the one on Gas Lane (Belmont Street).

Mr C. A. Smythe the company secretary, was quick to offer shares in the venture to any locals who were interested.

The project seemed beset by complications. At the beginning of 1911 the company name had changed to 'The Empire Theatre Syndicate, Manchester'. It had experienced difficulties obtaining a Dramatic Licence, and the ground had not been prepared for the proposed buildings.

★ ★ ★

The New Year had also brought problems for Edwin Lawrence and his travelling cinematograph show. He had made it through 1910 without the authorities causing him any undue worry. He realised this state of affairs would not continue for much longer.

On January 2nd in Ashby-de-la-Zouch misfortune struck the Lawrence camp when two reels of film were stolen.

From Ashby they moved on to Ibstock. Here, business was reasonable and they stayed until the end of the month. As the cold, grey daylight unfolded over Ibstock on the last day of January, Edwin and his crew pulled out. They were to make their way to Swadlincote via Ashby.

Disaster struck as they descended Alton Hill, 'Mikado', their Foster Showman's Engine, number 3036, made serious and expensive noises. An abrupt halt was followed by the sounds of groaning metal and splintering timber as the wagons behind the engine voiced their complaints. The contents spilled out, shattering on the road and embankment.

Miraculously Edwin and his companions, who had also been thrown in all directions were not hurt, with the exception of Joe Bachelor. Joe had been driving the engine and his foot was crushed between the wheel and footrest in the accident, resulting in screams of agony from the victim.

With the use of chains and blocks, and assistance from a passing tradesman and his horse, they eased the wheel and extricated Joe. He was made as comfortable as possible on the same tradesman's cart and accompanied to Ashby Cottage Hospital by two of the Lawrence Company.

The debris was cleared and the damage assessed. Repairs to 'Mikado' were carried out by a firm from Ashby. The trailers and vans were patched and made serviceable with the use of ropes, timber and nails.

A GRAND WRESTLING MATCH
will take place in
LAWRENCE'S EMPIRE, Swadlincote,
On FRIDAY, March 3rd, between
A. WOOD (of Linton) and SMITH (of Swad-
lincote).
Smith engages to throw Wood twice within
20 minutes.

All seats on this special night 4d. each; if
booked 6d.

The enterprising Edwin Lawrence Snr, gives up showing films for one night, 3rd March, 1911. Allowing his portable cinema, erected on Sabines Ground in Midland Road, to become the venue for a wrestling match. It was a sell out, Smith's prediction did not materialise. Wood of Linton secured three falls in 18 minutes, 40 seconds and claimed the match. (Burton Mail Archive).

Edwin Lawrence Snr, with family and friends, pose alongside 'MIKADO' their showman's traction engine. The location is thought to be Forest Gate, London, circa 1905. (D. Jamieson).

At mid-day on February 1st the battered land train of Edwin Lawrence and company pulled on to Sabines Ground in Midland Road, Swadlincote.

On the evening of Friday February 1st, The Empire Theatre and Hippodrome Company (Swadlincote) Ltd. held a meeting in the Nag's Head Hotel, Swadlincote. The name had been changed again but C. A. Smythe, the secretary, was still in the chair.

His approach was the same, and he was to be admired for the relentless way he campaigned to persuade his audience to purchase shares in the new theatre. Smythe said many had already invested capital in the project and, once the weather improved, work would begin preparing the ground prior to building.

Three gentlemen at the rear of the room listened to Smythe's eloquent sales-talk.

They were totally convinced the town needed a theatre or similar building, but they had been convinced of that before they entered the room.

Dressed in trilby hats and overcoats and smoking cigarettes, they were an imposing trio.

The eldest of them was Edwin Lawrence. The other two were Tommy Raynor and Frank Bridgewater, both of them a lot younger than Edwin.

Tommy's real name was Oliphant. He took the name Raynor from the act he had been part of in George Sanger's Circus. Sanger had retired from the road in 1905, and his circus disbanded and sold.

Tommy had continued to travel with different groups, exploiting his talents to earn a living, and learning others such as acting and an ability to master the new technology of the cinematograph. He had married Edwin's daughter Maude.

A few months earlier he had appeared in Swadlincote and decided to put down roots. When asked why he chose to live in a place which could only be described as an industrial battlefield, he replied: "I like the natives. They're the friendliest I've met". It was a statement he stood by until he died.

Frank Bridgewater was from Derby. His parents were thought to be publicans at 'The Old Crown Inn' on The Morledge. Frank had spent some time in America where he had been fascinated by the growth of the film industry.

During a conversation in his parents' hostelry, he mentioned to a customer his interest in cinematography. He expressed a wish to become involved in films or their making, believing it had a tremendous future.

The customer, a travelling showman, advised Frank to seek out a gentleman in Swadlincote by the name of Tommy Raynor. Raynor, according to the traveller, was well versed in the art of the moving picture and worth talking to.

Edwin Lawrence Jnr. Actor and comedian, who took part in the Swadlincote films, and also appeared on stage at the 'Alexandra Palace of Varieties'. His talent took him to the theatres in London's West End. He also took part in larger film productions, including 'The Midship Maid' which also starred John Mills and Jesse Mathews. (D. Jamieson).

Edwin Lawrence Snr. (J. Shorthouse).

Bridgewater followed the man's advice. He and Raynor quickly became friends and business partners. They purchased a projector and a screen, and rented films from a London company. These were delivered by rail to Swadlincote Station, and returned the same way, ensuring a swift and efficient change of programme.

An arrangement had been made with Ben Robinson to use the Alexandra Skating Rink on certain evenings for cinematograph shows, a licence having been granted by the local authorities for films to be shown there.

On the previous Tuesday (Feb 9th) they had given their first performance and it had been a resounding success.

They filed out from the 'Nags Head' meeting. Smythe was still talking to the few who were left. Edwin Lawrence glanced back at the chattering salesman, pausing for a moment, as if about to go back to tell Smythe something. Then he obviously thought better of it, and followed his two companions.

Edwin had spent many hours musing over his future since parking up in Swadlincote. He decided to sell most of his travelling show and equipment and settle down. By the beginning of March he had acquired a house in Swadlincote, Number 13 Weston Street.

His wife, Annie, vacated their premises in Forest Gate London, and travelled by train to her new home in South Derbyshire. Annie was his second wife. He had six children by his first marriage; Edwin (Jnr), Stanley, Maud, Alice, Morris and Fanny. Edwin and Annie would have two children in their Weston Street home, Edith and Conrad.

★ ★ ★

On March 23rd Lawrence announced his intentions to build an Electric Theatre in Swadlincote.

★ ★ ★

In June, Swadlincote Hippodrome and its contents went under the auctioneer's hammer and were sold.

Many rats sought other accommodation!

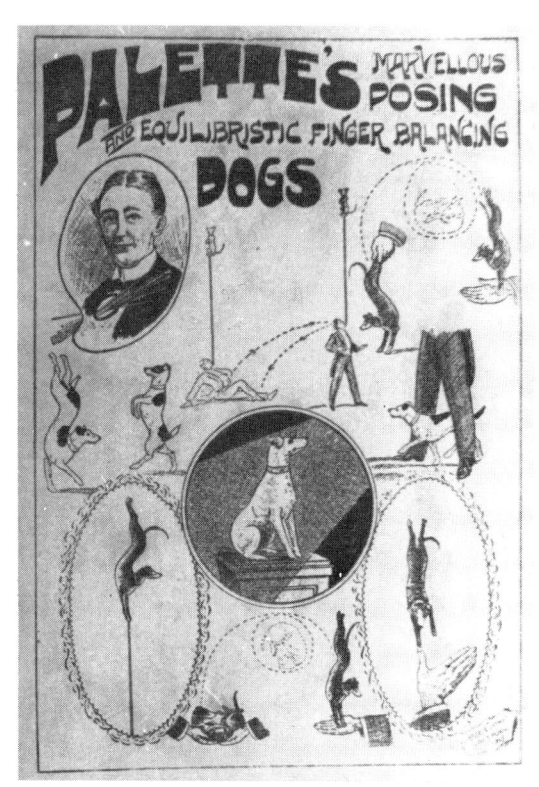

'PALETTE'. One of the many acts which appeared at the 'Alexandra Palace of Varieties'. (P. Palin).

Palette's
Original Canine Pot-Pourri Novelty.

In October Edwin Lawrence confirmed the purchase of a site in West Street, Swadlincote. He put forward plans for an elaborate, single-storey building, with arched entrances on either side, which would seat 500 customers. These were provisionally accepted.

ALEXANDRA PALACE of VARIETIES
SWADLINCOTE.
Engaged at Enormous Expense—
PALETTE,
And his marvellous Posing, Trick and Singer Equilibristic Balancing DOGS, in pot pourri music and lightning picture paintings, assisted by Mlle. HELENA. The last word in canine training.
Star Film—"HIS EVIL GENIUS."

A November, 1913 advertisement informing the populace of the appearance at enormous expense of 'PALETTE' and his performing dogs. (Burton Mail Archive).

The 'Empire Theatre', West Street, Swadlincote, opened its doors to the public for the first show on 26th December, 1912. It was demolished in the 1930s to make way for the 'New Empire'. To the right of the photograph is a kiln belonging to Sharpes Works. (M. McCann).

Percy McCann (left), with two unknown gentlemen, takes time out for a photograph at the front of the 'Empire'. The prices of admission are clearly marked on the separate pay boxes. The 'Special Notice', in the centre of the photograph, warns the patrons; 'Should this theatre have to close through any unforeseen circumstance created by the war. No money will be refunded! (M. McCann).

The cinematograph shows at the Alexandra Rink grew in popularity, now on two nights each week, Tuesday and Thursday.

On skating nights at the Rink another face became familiar, that of a well-dressed young man, well-mannered, small in stature, he rarely skated, but walked around the outskirts of the proceedings. The well-sprung polished floor finished in Canadian Sugar Maple seemed to fascinate him and he would constantly slide his shoes across it as if he were about to start dancing.

As far as the rink was concerned, its use for dancing was out of the question. In 1910 permission was granted by the local court for a band to be in attendance for certain skating occasions. It was granted on the strict understanding that the building could not be used as a dancing saloon. This did nothing to deter the young man's dreams. His name was Ernest Hall.

Edwin moved into action, having the site in West Street cleared for his new venture. He came under constant criticism and attack from religious groups and others in the hierarchy of Swadlincote. Their constant verbal offensive on him, both in and out of court, was perhaps his reason, or one of his reasons, for abandoning the project in mid-1912.

WEST STREET, SWADLINCOTE.

West Street, Swadlincote, looking towards High Street, circa 1907. The Empire Theatre was eventually built on the right, almost opposite the Wesleyan Chapel. (T. Gardner).

Another view of West Street, Swadlincote. By now the original Empire Theatre had been replaced by the much larger New Empire. One prospective customer checks out the programmes on offer before returning to his bicycle, leaning against the bus stop and gas lamp. (T Gardner).

He still had an ace to play along with Raynor and Bridgewater.
C. A. Smythe and his plans seemed to have drifted into oblivion.

Thomas Henry Taylor (Harry). Resplendent in the uniform of a Burton hospital porter (early 1900s). He took part in the early Swadlincote films and eventually became the projectionist at the 'Alexandra Palace of Varieties'. In later years he was employed at the Empire and Majestic cinemas in Swadlincote. (R Taylor).

Tommy Oliphant (alias Raynor), circus acrobat turned actor, film-maker and cinema proprietor, circa 1913. (D. Jamieson).

Within a week of Edwin abandoning his proposals, a group of businessmen, spearheaded by one Charles Garibaldi McCann from Derby, took up the campaign to build an Electric Theatre in Swadlincote. It was to be erected on land adjacent to the Lawrence site on West Street.

McCann was the main shareholder in the organisation, which also included individuals from Derby and Swadlincote. After selling his musical instrument shop, near 'The Spot' in Derby, he opened a similar business in Swadlincote High Street. The family, including his son Percy, settled in the district and were to have a long association with local cinema.

McCann and his associates received similar condemnation to Lawrence, but before the close of 1912 they had succeeded in building a theatre.

One protester's opinion was that the Devil had got his own way in allowing a Picture Palace to be built so close to a house of God.

On Boxing day the Swadlincote Entertainments Co. Ltd. opened The New Empire Picture Palace in West Street, Swadlincote.

Top of the bill was Miss Winnie Southgate, singer, dancer and comedienne, along with Knowles and Bowles performing ragtime dancing and dialogue sketches. They were supported by films including 'White Treachery' (an Indian Adventure) and Topsy's Dream of Toyland. The latter, being a story of a child at Christmas, was appropriate for the time of the year.

Charles McCann's music shop near to the 'Spot' in Derby, before he moved to Swadlincote, where he opened a similar shop and became heavily involved in the cinema business. (M. McCann).

Percy McCann (at the wheel), cinema manager and automobile owner, with his family outside their home in Weston Street, Swadlincote. (M. McCann).

During the day the Empire played to three full houses, packing them in on the velvet tip-up seats in the sixpenny section and the leather-covered benches in the threepennies. After a few hiccups on the films Mr Crawley quickly mastered the operation of the Pathe cinematograph equipment. Throughout the following week the programme changed each day, and the Empire was packed to capacity—500 people—for each show.

Local purveyors of entertainment, on seeing the impact the Empire made, may have wondered what the future held for them. Perhaps some even rushed to Scholefields chemists and purchased a box of Doctor Williams Pink Pills for Pale People, or drowned their sorrows in pints of Eadies Ale served up by Tom Whitehall at the Market Inn.

Others, however, carried on in their usual vein. Ernest Hall continued to organise dances throughout the area, and Mr Poyser was still the town's most popular disc-jockey, providing entertainment in local hostelries with his new gramophone and records.

The Alexandra Skating Rink continued to roll along, but the pace was beginning to slow. Roller skating had passed its peak, and many rinks were closing or being converted for other uses.

For Raynor, Bridgewater and Lawrence this was a lucky break. They had already built up a reputation with their cinematograph shows. After consultation with Ben Robinson and the local authorities, they came up with a more ambitious plan.

A partition wall was built at the far end of the rink. Beyond it the space was converted into a hall suitable for presenting variety acts and cinema shows. Entry to the hall was from Bank Passage. A raised floor was assembled above the existing floor, the highest point being against the wall opposite the entrance—the wall nearest to Wraggs Yard.

On the outside of this wall was built the projectionist's compartment. At the other end was the stage and screen, with the entrance and paybox set to one side. The building could hold over 300 customers. It was named 'The Alexandra Palace of Varieties'.

The Alexandra became a serious competitor for the Empire. Raynor and Lawrence had many contacts in the entertainment world, and were quick to bring in a wide variety of acts from many different places. Edwin Lawrence Jnr. was also making a name for himself as a comedian. He, too, would pass on acts to the Alexandra and often appeared there himself.

The electrics required for projectors and lighting were arranged by local man William Lilley, who eventually became Chief Engineer on the Burton and Ashby Light Railway.

A building was erected near the Alexandra Rink to house the generating equipment.

A horizontal single cylinder diesel engine, of unknown parentage, supplied the power to propel a flywheel exceeding 10 feet in diameter. A deep groove was cut into the floor of the building to accommodate the monster. A quick release handle, which did not always live up to its name, slotted into the side of the wheel. The handle allowed two people to rotate the giant, whilst another operated the decompressor on the engine.

Once it was felt the wheel was turning at a reasonable speed, one of the team would give the signal to leap clear. The decompression lever was let go, and all three would flatten themselves against the walls as the whole apparatus shook and shuddered into life.

Those who took part in, or witnessed, this operation, claimed it was more frightening than anything seen on the cinema screen.

Not only did the generator supply power to the Rink and Theatre, but for a short time also produced electricity which was sold to a number of shops in the High Street.

As the enterprise grew Walter Smith, who lived at the rear of the Post Office in West Street, helped out as a projectionist. If he was not available Henry 'Harry' Taylor would take over.

Harry eventually left his job as a hospital porter and was employed full-time in local cinemas for the rest of his working life.

Frank Bridgewater was an accomplished pianist and provided music for artistes and the silent films.

By mid-1913 reports in the local press were full of praise for the entertainment and packed houses at The Alexandra.

It was now that Raynor, Bridgewater and Lawrence played their ace.

Behind the scenes. A photograph taken outside the 'Alexandra Palace of Varieties' projectionists box and cutting room. The unknown helper on the right carries an empty spool, whilst Jim Smith (left), holds a reel full of entertainment. Harry Taylor (centre), seems to have performed an act of censorship on the forthcoming programme. (R. Taylor).

Film Fun

During his travelling days Edwin had become proficient not only in the art of showing films, but also in making them. He had worked closely with the Holland family, whose descendants still bring their travelling funfair to Gresley Common.

The arrangement between the two groups was as follows. Edwin, accompanied by one or two of the Holland camp, would position a movie camera at the gates of factories or workplaces in towns they were about to visit. The workforce of the establishments would be filmed going into or leaving work.

When the fairground cinema was erected in the town, a sign would be placed at the entrance: 'See yourself on the Silver Screen'. It was a ploy used for many years.

Edwin had also made films in his own right at Forest Gate, his old base in London.

It is likely they were bought and distributed by firms in the capital. One early film attributed to Edwin was entitled, 'The Little Flower Girl and The Fighting Parson'.

★ ★ ★

It was Saturday August 23rd, 1913.

The football field close to Oversetts Road, Newhall, was a scene of colour, noise and excitement. The commotion was brought about by the Swadlincote Parade, and the bands and exhibits, which numbered almost 90, had gathered on the field. Underfoot, the ground was still damp from the previous day's heavy rain. The morning had started with similar threats from the overcast sky, but by 10 'o clock it had cleared, and held promise of a bright summer day.

The organisers, led by Mr T. Parker (J.P.) of Woodville and Mr T. H. Warren, were more than pleased with the turnout. Entries included Halls Collieries, Albion Clay, Robinson and Dowlers Works, Salt and Co's Brewery and, at the other end of the scale, Mr Oakley (Chimney Sweep) and Mr F. Richardson's decorated cycle.

Mingled with these were half a dozen brass and silver bands, and a similar number of comic bands including Harry Harper's Ragtime Pupils (the pride of Albert village).

Mrs Jack Moir, along with a group of dedicated workers, had succeeded in selling thousands of imitation marguerites, the flower chosen for 1913. The proceeds from these, and other money raised by the parade, would be distributed between local hospitals and nursing charities.

Once the task of judging had been completed the procession hit the road. Like a giant, colourful snake it meandered through Newhall, Midway and Gresley, full of music, shouting and laughter, winding

Annie Holland and company 'take a breather' somewhere in Lincolnshire. Supplies of water and coal for 'CHALLENGER', their showman's traction engine, must have caused a few headaches at times. No such problems with the horses pulling the living van at the rear of this land train, a grass verge and stream are all that is required. (B. Holland).

Holland's 'Palace of Light'. Assembled shortly after delivery, the location is believed to be Mount Sorrel. Annie Holland and family proudly pose for a photograph on their new acquisition. This early fairground cinema would visit many towns and cities in the Midlands. In later years the Hollands family built and operated 'The Empire' cinema, at Measham. (B. Holland).

between clay banks, spoil heaps, kilns and smoking chimneys, that were forgotten for the day.

Eventually the cavalcade filed into a field adjacent to Midland Road. Here it came to a halt. More entertainment ensued from various bands and choirs.

The day closed with a spectacular firework display. Many left with memories to last a lifetime.

Raynor, Bridgewater and Lawrence had taken memories a step further and produced a film of the parade.

★ ★ ★

The programme at The Alexandra Palace of Varieties the following Monday (August 25) included Florina Cody (Sharp Shooting Prairie Girl), Mark Leo (Comedian) and Douglas and Gordon (Scottish Singers and Dancers). Films included 'The Counterfeiters', 'The Foiling of The Five Fiends', 'Their Idols' and 'Doggies Debut', but the one which attracted the crowd was 'The Swadlincote Parade'. It was publicised to the maximum by using the phrase 'Come and see yourself on the Silver Screen'.

A report in The Burton Daily mail the following day said this about the show—'Every available seat was occupied last night and the efforts of the proprietors to put the best in front of their large crowd of patrons were

The horse-drawn float of Robinson and Dowler Limited, displaying their products and complete with a chimney sweep! One of the many entrants in the 1913 Swadlincote Parade, captured on movie film, and shown at the 'Alexandra Palace of Varieties'. (P. M. White).

heartily appreciated. The picture is very clear, and the parade exhibits are easily recognisable'.

Customers by now had a fantastic choice of entertainment. Charles McCann and his associates at The Empire were formidable competition. They also produced excellent programmes of variety acts and films for the clientele, changing the shows in mid-week.

The Alexandra also changed programme on Thursdays. Those locals able to afford it could see four different shows every week.

An even wider choice was almost achieved when McCann applied to build a cinema in Newhall, but the authorities refused his plans.

★ ★ ★

To Lawrence, filming the parade was child's play. Raynor, Bridgewater and Edwin had already made more ambitious plans concerning film making.

They formed 'The Albion Film Company', believing that, in the near future, they would employ large numbers of people in the film-making business.

Their first move in this direction was to produce a full length film locally. It was called 'The Plumber and the Lunatics'. The production was to cause a great deal of free entertainment, and was described as follows in the columns of the 'Burton Gazette'

ALEXANDRA PALACE of VARIETIES,
SWADLINCOTE
TO-NIGHT—THE SWADLINCOTE PARADE
Come and see Yourself on the Pictures.
"THE COUNTERFEITERS."
FLORINA CODY, the Prairie Girl Rifle Shot
MARK LEO, Comedian.

Lawrence, Raynor and Bridgewater, filmed the 1913 Swadlincote Parade. The advertisement uses a phrase which would guarantee a full house at the 'Alexandra Palace of Varieties'. 'Come and see yourself on the pictures'. (Burton Mail Archives).

ALEXANDRA PALACE of VARIETIES,
SWADLINCOTE
TO-NIGHT—THE PLUMBER & THE LUNATIC
See the First Local Production.
"LADY AUDLEY'S SECRET."
LES CERATTES, Vocalists & Specialty Dancers.
FRED CHARLIER, Comedy Magician.

The first full length local film was a comedy. 'The Plumber and the Lunatics', even though the latter in this Burton Gazette advertisement from September 1913 is in the singular. (Burton Mail Archives).

The Plumber and the Lunatics

The information is taken from the Burton Gazette Local Chit-Chat columns from Friday 22nd August, to Thursday 28th August 1913.

When the residents of the local colliery district observed the words "County Asylum" painted in large letters on the yard door of the Nag's Head Inn, mild consternation naturally prevailed, and when a man with a wild and dangerous look in his eyes was seen to dash out of the yard, hotly pursued by two other men—one with a formidable knife in his hand, the curiosity aroused was considerable. The fugitive climbed on the roof of the Skating Rink, still closely followed, then descended into a field at the rear of Sharpe Brothers works, afterwards taking to the roof of Messrs May and Tills printing works. Just as a few of the spectators were beginning to shake off their amazement, and the exciting chase looked like being rudely interrupted—with perhaps drastic consequences for his pursuers—a small boy espied a man, in an inconspicious position, slowly turning the handle of a camera. The boy shouted "cinema"—and the truth was out.

It afterwards transpired that Messrs Raynor and Bridgewater, the proprietors of the Alexandra Palace of Varieties, were engaged in producing a comedy, the plot of which in brief was as follows—A plumber is called to repair a gas leak at the Asylum. Standing at the top of a ladder he lets fall his knife, and is alarmed to find that two of the inmates have taken possession of the weapon. He falls from the ladder and runs for his life, chased in the manner we have already described, by the lunatics. Yesterday the chase finished in High Street Swadlincote from where it will be continued in a day or so. After Part of the photoplay has been enacted in Ashby the chase will be concluded in the River Trent at Stapenhill. The plumber will enter a boat and row out to the middle of the river, followed by the pursuers, who will also attempt to enter the boat. Of course this capsizes, and the three men struggle in the water. All that happens after this is the handing over of the gruesome weapon, with all of the politeness imaginable to the amazed plumber, who was unaware of the kindly intention of the men, who had chased him so persistently. The role of the plumber was filled by Mr Raynor himself while Mr Bridgewater took that of a lunatic. It is rumoured that the Swadlincote Skating Rink will shortly be converted into a cinematograph studio, where other local pictures will be produced, giving employment to between 100 and 200 local people.

August 27th 1913, Local Chit-Chat

The final stage of the cinematograph film, the enacting of which was started at Swadlincote on Thursday, afforded a good deal of amusement to pedestrians on the Stapenhill Viaduct on Tuesday afternoon.

> ALEXANDRA PALACE of VARIETIES
> SWADLINCOTE.
>
> TO-NIGHT—"A NOBLE BROTHER," the great poaching picture, produced in South Derbyshire.
> "THE WAYWARD WOMAN."
> ARTISTES—:
> TOM BURTON (comedian); IDA CONROY (soprano).

'A Noble Brother', was a more dramatic production. It was filmed in Swadlincote and also in the more picturesque settings along the Repton Brook and Bretby Park. (Burton Mail Archives).

Empire Theatre WEST STREET, SWADLINCOTE

PICTURES AND VARIETIES.

Doors Open 6-15 to 10-15.

TWO DISTINCT PERFORMANCES

EVERY SATURDAY, 6 o'clock and 8 o'clock.

SPECIAL MATINEE at Two o'clock.

PROPRIETOR - - - CHAS. McCANN.
Willsons, Nottm.

An Advertising card for the 'Empire Theatre', Swadlincote, circa 1913. (M. McCann).

As already outlined, the Stapenhill scenes partook of the nature of an aquatic carnival and included a battle royal between two of Mr. Dobson's boats. Promptly at three o' clock a wild eyed individual dashed from the rear of the boat sheds, where by the way, he had been waiting for some ten minutes and hurriedly leaping into the boat pushed off into the middle of the river. A moment later he was followed by two other men, who in another craft, went in hot pursuit. A wrestling match in mid-river took place, with the inevitable result of the upsetting of the three actors into the water. When once on dry land the plumber for such was the fugitive was most polietly presented by the pursuers with a formidable knife they were carrying. Unfortunately at that juncture, a couple of asylum warders appeared and arrested the polite ones, for it appeared that they were polite lunatics.

The camera operator was situated just beyond the boat sheds in order to include the bridge and the lower portion of the river in his view.

The Ferry Bridge crosses the Trent at Stapenhill. This was the setting chosen for the aquatic finale to the locally produced film, 'The Plumber and the Lunatics'. (Valentines Postcard - G. Nutt).

Gazette Thursday August 28th, Local Chit-Chat

As already indicated the Swadlincote Public have had a new and fascinating amusement provided for them—that of watching the antics of cinema actors. It is unnecessary to dilate upon the popularity of the innovating and the spectators are quite unanimous that it is far better in real life than on the screen. Messrs. Raynor and Bridgewater are quite outstanding features in the mining district just at present, and can be sure of a following of youngsters, who, remaining at a discreet distance, yet hope to see some of the fun attendant on cinema acting.

In order to ensure the complete success of the first film entirely constructed locally, additional scenes were added on Wednesday in the Ashby Cattle Market, while this morning the actors disported themselves in the yard of the Nag's Head Inn, and delighted the spectators by their caperings under the influence of a strong jet of water. It is stated that the film will be shown in Swadlincote on Monday next. Mr. Raynor has taken the part of the plumber, Messrs. Bridgewater and Lawrence have proved most capable lunatics, while the zeal manifested by Messrs. H. Taylor and S. Slym has also been gratifying.

The movie makers continued by making impromptu snatches of film featuring members of the South Derbyshire population.

One gentleman was supposedly run over by a road roller. His flattened remains, which were really a large cardboard replica, were pulled from beneath the vehicle.

The Alexandra shook with laughter when a film clip containing a steady procession of 40 or more well known locals, emerging from a single barrel, was shown.

Another scene portrayed a rather overweight Mr. Beech, Turf Accountant of West Street. He was presumed to be swimming the English Channel, but once again it was the tricks of the camera. The filming took place in the reservoir at the rear of Sharpe's works in West Street.

Mr. Beech had obviously been a good sport and allowed a rope to be tied around his person with which other locals pulled him across the pool at an alarming rate of knots. More folk created waves by splashing long lengths of timber in the water.

★ ★ ★

Their next full-length film was to be more dramatic. It was entitled 'A Noble Brother'. The storyline involved two brothers, one on the side of the law in the guise of a prison officer and the other a criminal. The latter was placed by mistake, in the group of convicts his brother was guarding. One of the prisoners attempted to escape by attacking the guard, but the criminal brother intervened and saved the day. All ended happily when, because of his noble deed, he was pardoned and released.

Again the district and its population were utilized to the full.

The rear of a house in Stanhope Road was used, in a setting depicting a burglar forcing the french windows in an effort to break in.

The following scene of the thief within the house was created inside the Alexandra Skating Rink. The Albion Film Company had ideas of using the Rink as a full-time studio. Raynor had removed a number of roof panels and replaced them with glass to allow in more light. They hoped this would improve conditions for film-making inside the Rink.

A house in Hearthcote Road, served as a courthouse, and scenes of drunkards in a gambling den were created in 'The Granville Arms' next to the Delph.

The role of a poacher was handed to the local legend of the long-net, Charles Hextall.

Charles had made numerous appearances in the local court accused of poaching. His verbal sparring with those on the bench caused amazement at the expense of the magistrates, but in turn left a dent in Hextall's pocket.

On one occasion he had been accused of taking rabbits from an area close to Lea Wood.

"I could not have taken any rabbits from there, sir", insisted Charles.

"And how can you be so sure about that?" retorted the magistrate.

"Because I took them all from there three years ago," replied the smiling defendant.

The courtroom erupted in laughter and cheering, the public clearly on Charles' side.

Despite his unpopularity with the law and landowners, he was well liked and respected by the local working class. Many of them would be given rabbits or similar fayre, by Charles Hextall if they fell on hard times.

He accepted the role of film star provided his friend Joe Fletcher was included in the cast. This was agreed.

Camera, cameraman and the cast were also to be found on the outskirts of Bretby Park. Dogs, accompanied by actors portraying a gamekeeper and policemen, chased Charles Hextall, carrying two expired rabbits, across the countryside.

They pursued him down a hill and Charles plunged into a lake. The idea was for the dogs to follow him, but they refused and took up an uninterested pose at the water's edge. It was left to those acting as officers of the law to take part in the aquatic arrest of Charles Hextall.

The film was first shown on Monday October 13th, 1913, and the following report was found in the local newspaper the following day—

Burton Evening Gazette Tuesday October 14th 1913

Local Chit-Chat—It has now been proved beyond doubt that there is in South Derbyshire some of the best possible scenery for the production of cinema films. This was more than emphasised last night when 'A Noble Brother', enacted principally by local talent on the borders of Bretby Park, and in various haunts in Swadlincote and District was shown at the Alexandra. The interest taken in the picture by a crowded house was delightful to witness. Here and there everyone were straining their necks to catch a glimpse of everything that was to be seen. The enthusiasm which prevailed throughout the exhibition of the film, which is 2,250 ft. in length, must have been encouraging to Messrs. Raynor and Bridgewater, who are to be complimented in taking the lead and showing the public that it is possible to take some of the best pictures in their own district. As for the picture itself one could have desired for nothing better, as apart from the local interest, there were incidents which thrilled and those which caused shrieks of laughter. At one there was to be seen a gambling den in a local hostelry and at another period local poachers were struggling desperately with the police on the outskirts of Bretby Park. It would take up too much space to give in detail one half of what happens, but those who desire to see the first dramatic picture taken in the district are assured of twenty minutes delight while 'A Noble Brother' is being shown.

Was Swadlincote set to become another Elstree or Pinewood?

Charles Hextall (far right), former film star! In later years with a group of friends, on the yard of the 'Masons Arms', Midway, and still the joker. Wherever did those fish come from? (S. Mewis).

An older Joe Fletcher, friend of Charles Hextall, who appeared alongside him in the local film 'A Noble Brother'. (D. Garrett).

Tommy Oliphant (alias Raynor), postpones his career as a cinema proprietor, film producer and actor, and volunteers to fight in the First World War. (D. Jamieson).

Charles Hextall, volunteered for the armed forces, exchanging his hunting grounds of Bretby and Hartshorne for the French battlefields where he served as a farrier. (S. Mewis).

The Empire and Alexandra went from strength to strength, both playing to packed houses, through Christmas and into 1914.

During January vandals caused havoc in the Alexandra Rink and cinema, smashing fittings and pouring paint indiscriminately throughout the premises. Despite the difficulties this caused, business carried on as usual.

On Wednesday, January 21, the local Conservative Party held a successful whist drive and dance in the Alexandra Skating Rink. The local court's decision to ban dancing in the Rink had been brushed aside and would continue to be so for decades to come.

This did not go unnoticed by Ernest Hall.

Film clips were still being made locally, but no more full-length feature films were produced.

Perhaps the film makers argued amongst themselves.

Perhaps the owners of the Rink did not share their enthusiasm for film-making.

Whatever the reasons, many lives, families and businesses were about to undergo enormous changes following the outbreak of The First World War. Many local men were about to exchange the clayholes of South Derbyshire for the shellholes and mud of the French battlefields.

For those who were lucky enough to return, and these would include volunteers such as Raynor and Hextall, life would never be quite the same.

But that's another story. . .

> It's Charlie this, and Charlie that
> And Charlie is a brute,
> But Charlie is a hero when the
> Guns begin to shoot.
>   (Slightly 'poached' Kipling).

Also available from Trent Valley Publications:

A Pictorial Record of the Leicester and Burton Branch Railway.

The second Trent Valley title from Nelson Twells, who is well known for his interest in the LMS, and local Railway history, this book gives the history of a branch railway which not only connected the towns of Beer and Lace, but travelled through a variety of industrial and rural settings on its route. In addition to a journey first along the original West Bridge line, and then returning to Leicester for a trip through the delightfully sounding Kirby Muxloe, Desford, Coalville and Ashby De La Zouch to Burton on Trent, and round the Swadlincote loop, there are working timetables, maps, and a host of other information. Over 200 photographs are used to bring the line to life.

96pp A4